SACRED GROUND

Photos and Text by
David Kline

Acknowledgements

A special thanks to Gary Gardiner, Photo Editor,
Associated Press, Columbus, Ohio Bureau, who gave me a start
in photojournalism over a decade ago. To Pam Sloan of
by deSign who helped with the design of the book.
Also thank you to a former combat Marine,
Myke Henderly, for sharing with us his deep feelings on the
Vietnam Memorial and the Vietnam War through his poetry.
Finally, thanks to my wife, Dr. Jennifer Kline, for
standing by me with her love and understanding.

Dedication

*Dedicated to my father, Russell B. Kline, who passed
away before this journey was completed.*

PREFACE

We have all viewed on TV or in newspapers, books and magazines, the wreckage of war... a burned-out tank or A.P.C. along a red dusty road; a shot-up helicopter, its blades askew, resting in a rice paddy; spent shell casings; bloody dressings; battle gear; or mangled bodies lying in some far off outpost after a fierce battle. But the real wreckage of war... I viewed through my camera lens as I visited the most emotional place on earth today, the grounds of the Vietnam Veterans' Memorial in Washington, D.C.

As a photojournalist, I am in the business of photographing faces on a daily basis, but I have never seen faces like I have seen in the times I have been to the memorial over the years. We, as veterans, are familiar with the thousand yard stare, but this goes beyond that. These expressions and emotions were on the faces of family members, survivors, friends and buddies of the 58,000 plus names on the wall. They were all still carrying the trauma of this war that ended over two decades ago. In later years, as I looked through my loupe on a light table at the negatives, I saw these same faces staring at me, haunting me. These faces have been the driving force in putting this book together.

These are the faces of people whose lives were changed forever; who have these memories burned into their souls until it is their time to leave this earth. When they are at these "Sacred Grounds", the Vietnam Veterans' Memorial, these memories are more alive than ever. The pictures need no captions. They speak for themselves.

The Gold Star Mother reaching, as if reaching into the wall to touch her son; a wheelchair-bound survivor staring into the black granite with perhaps memories of some fierce jungle firefight or a night ambush gone bad; a Marine's blank stare remembering a rocket, mortar attack, buddies dying, trying to crawl closer into the earth, feeling like an elephant was sitting on his chest, unable to breathe, thinking the incoming rounds would never stop; a nurse's distant expression, maybe going back in time, a time of too many dustoffs, too many bloody young faces. A mother thinking of her son's first step, knowing he's now gone forever; a father of his son's first Little League home run, a wife or girlfriend, of their first kiss, their senior prom together. The young man or woman (now about the same age as the forever-young men on the wall) wondering about the father they never got to know.

The battles and gunfire are long since over, but war still lives in the souls of these people.

This is not meant in any way to be an anti-war book or a book against the Vietnam War. However, if a politician, on the eve of casting a vote to go to war, or some general, before sending young men and women to some far off place to wage war, could look at the wreckage of war in the faces I have seen two decades after a war has ended... maybe they would stop and ponder the consequences. I hope they will.

David Kline
Photojournalist and Vietnam Veteran

INSIDE THE WALL

I wonder if I died in vain,
will someone come and trace my name?
I didn't leave too much behind,
just relatives I couldn't find.

I never had a mom or dad,
Marines were all the friends I had.
Now most of them are in here too,
this wall's the home I never knew.

Rows and rows of names etched in stone
and yet I still feel I'm alone.
So many people come and cry,
but all their thoughts just pass me by.

It's tough to be an orphan child,
you try your best but no one's proud.
Thank God my buddies came with me
Although we're dead, we're family.

       C. Mykel Henderly

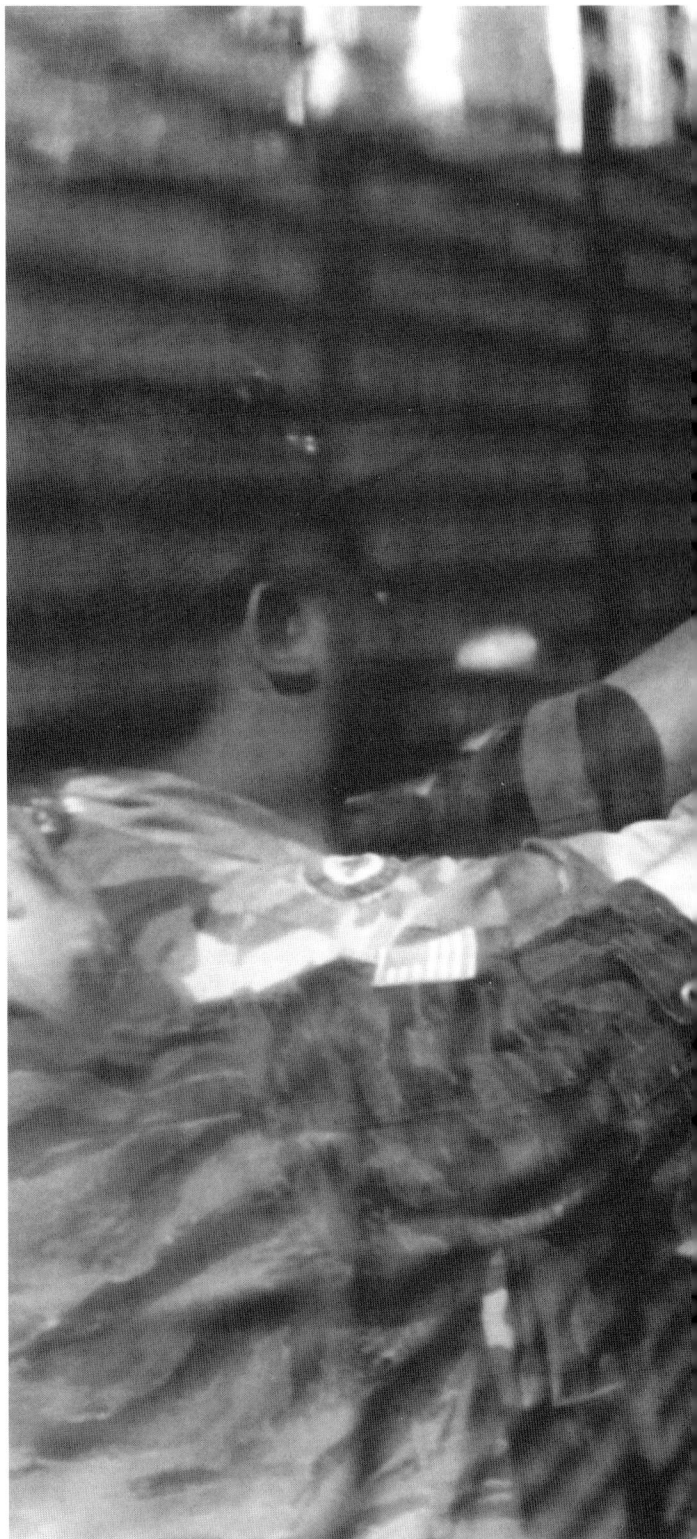

No experience in life is more terrifying or as brutal as war. Any war. The scars and memories linger. . . perhaps cloaked in silence as we go on with everyday life, but forever burned into our mind and soul.

The Vietnam War was different from other wars, not more brutal or more terrifying, but different. Fought by young adults who'd come of age during the era of John Wayne, JFK's New Frontier and the Age of Aquarius. This was a war without clear objectives. A war with no winners. . . only losers.

Vietnam veterans didn't come home to entertain the local folks with their "war stories of heroism" as in the past; they didn't want to talk about it. That suited most people - they wanted to forget it; politicians wanted it to go away. It was only with friends who were there, other vets, and usually on a night of drinking, that the stories were told. Only veterans cared about other veterans; no one else.

Then came the wall. The Vietnam Memorial in Washington, D.C., a project of Vietnam veteran Jan Scruggs, was definitely different. Its unveiling was clouded by controversy. Some rejected it, some called it the "black wall of shame" because of its unusual design, and still others felt they were dealt another unfair slice of life. Their monument was going to be as controversial as the war itself. But for me and for the hundreds, sometimes thousands, who visit daily, that black wall has become the most emotional and moving memorial in the world.

I remember the year the wall was dedicated, I watched the ceremony on television with the scores of veterans parading in their jungle fatigues decorated with medals, patches and slogans. Something stirred within me. I wanted to be a part of this.

My first visit to the memorial was in 1984, when the Statue of Soldiers was unveiled. It was also my first visit to Washington, D.C., a vacation. In my cloak of buried memories, I recall being more interested in seeing the Capitol than the memorial.

A veteran wearing an old-time black Cavalry hat gave me directions to the wall. As I headed out, this former Air Cavalry helicopter pilot cautioned me, "You had better get a hold of yourself." I assured him, and knew myself, that I was OK, just eager to see the wall.

Little did I know I was on my way to the beginning of some of the most emotional peaks and valleys I had ever experienced in my life.

On that unusually mild November night, I arrived at this very black monument stuck in the ground like a walk-out cellar and surrounded by the greenest grass. It was spooky.

Within minutes, an overpowering blackness seemed to envelope me, a feeling of depression and hopelessness of a magnitude I had never and have never since experienced. Seeing all the names was like being at a thousand funerals at once.

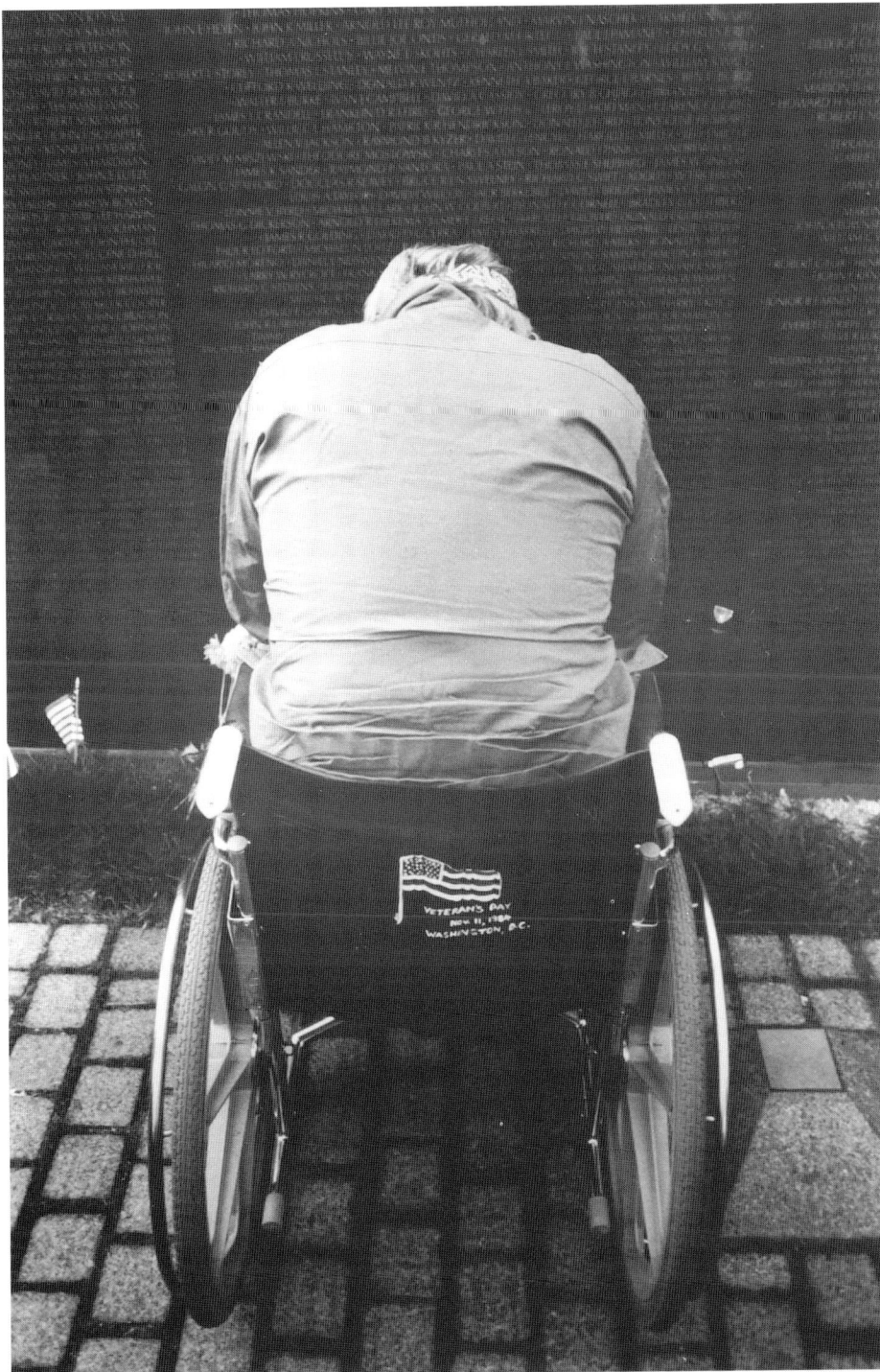

It all became a blur. I am a photographer, and yet I took no pictures, I wanted only to escape, to get in my car and leave.

That would have been the biggest mistake of my life.

I knew I had to see it again, but inwardly I struggled against it. After a restless night, I forced myself out into the bright sunlight of a warm November day to revisit the blackness.

This time there was a huge crowd, not just a few people here and there as the evening before. On the path to the wall, a former 1st Air Cav platoon leader started my personal healing process.

Dressed in jungle fatigues with lieutenant bars, he saw the 1st Air Cavalry patch on my faded fatigue jacket, grabbed my hand and said simply, "Welcome home, brother."

As the day wore on, the black feeling subsided, replaced by a new inner peace. I was among people like myself, with feelings like mine, all brought together by a long slab of black granite filled with all those names of fallen soldiers. It was as if the dead had beckoned us all to be there together now, as we had been together then.

The Wall is personal.
Some people suffer in
silence with blank stares.

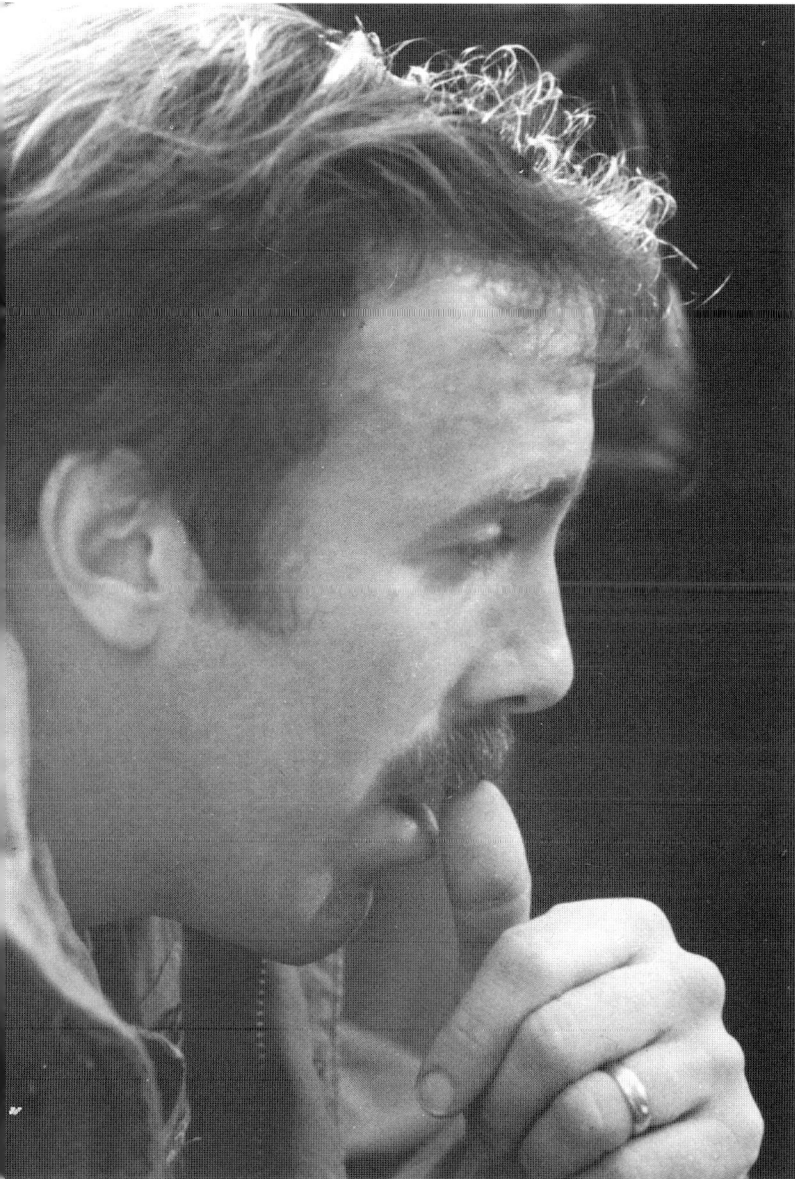

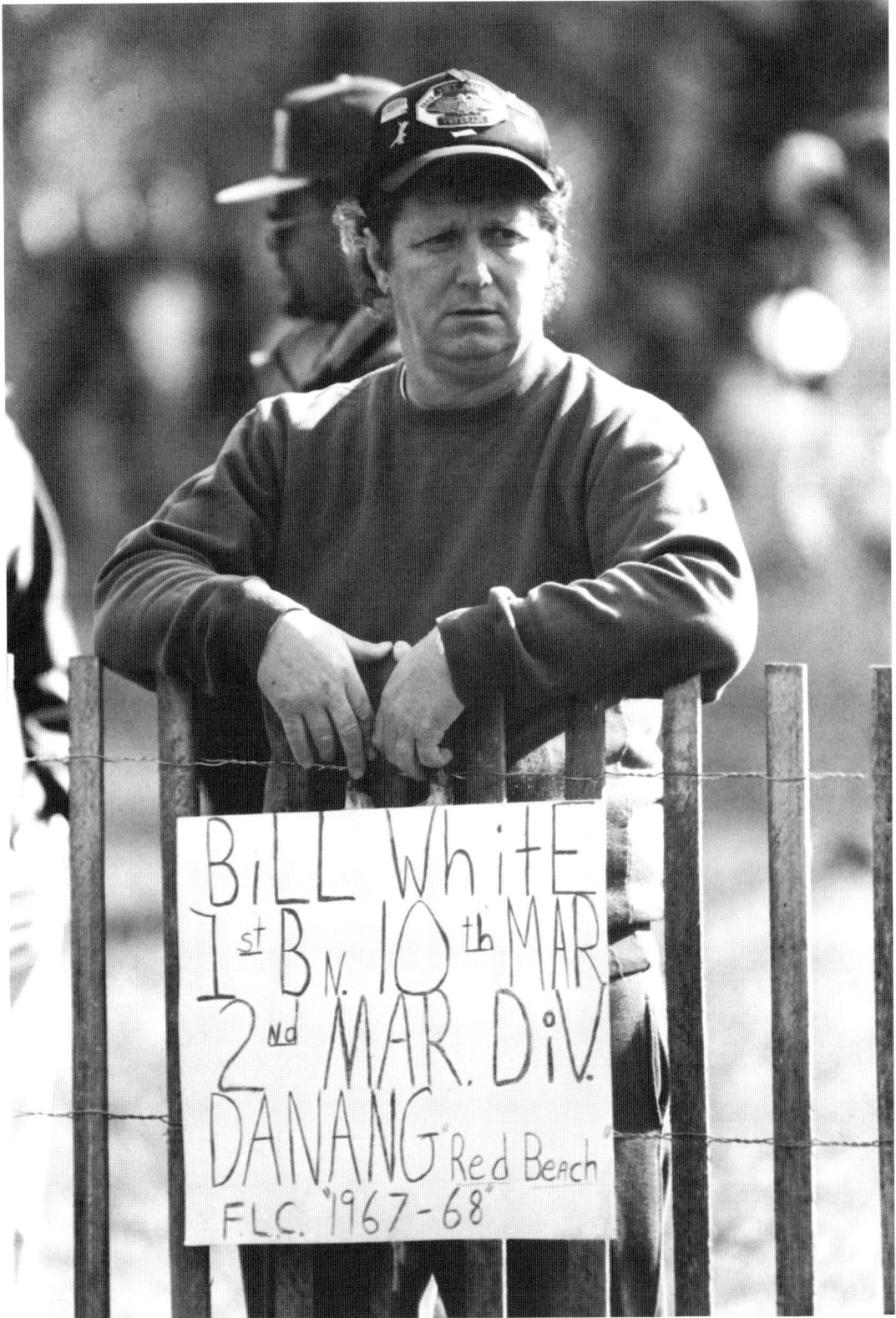

BILL WHITE
1st BN. 10th MAR.
2nd MAR. DIV.
DANANG "Red Beach"
F.L.C. "1967-68"

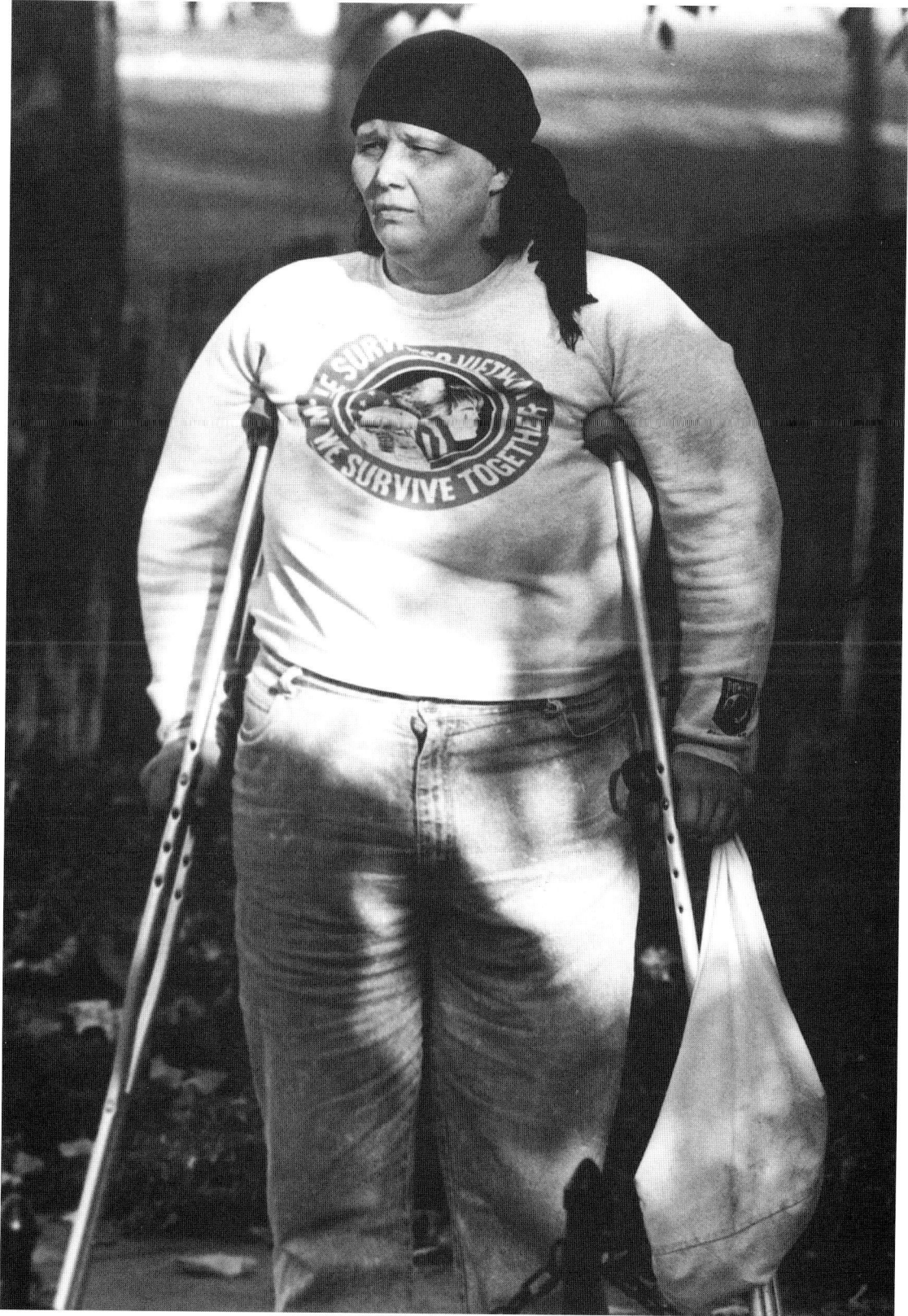

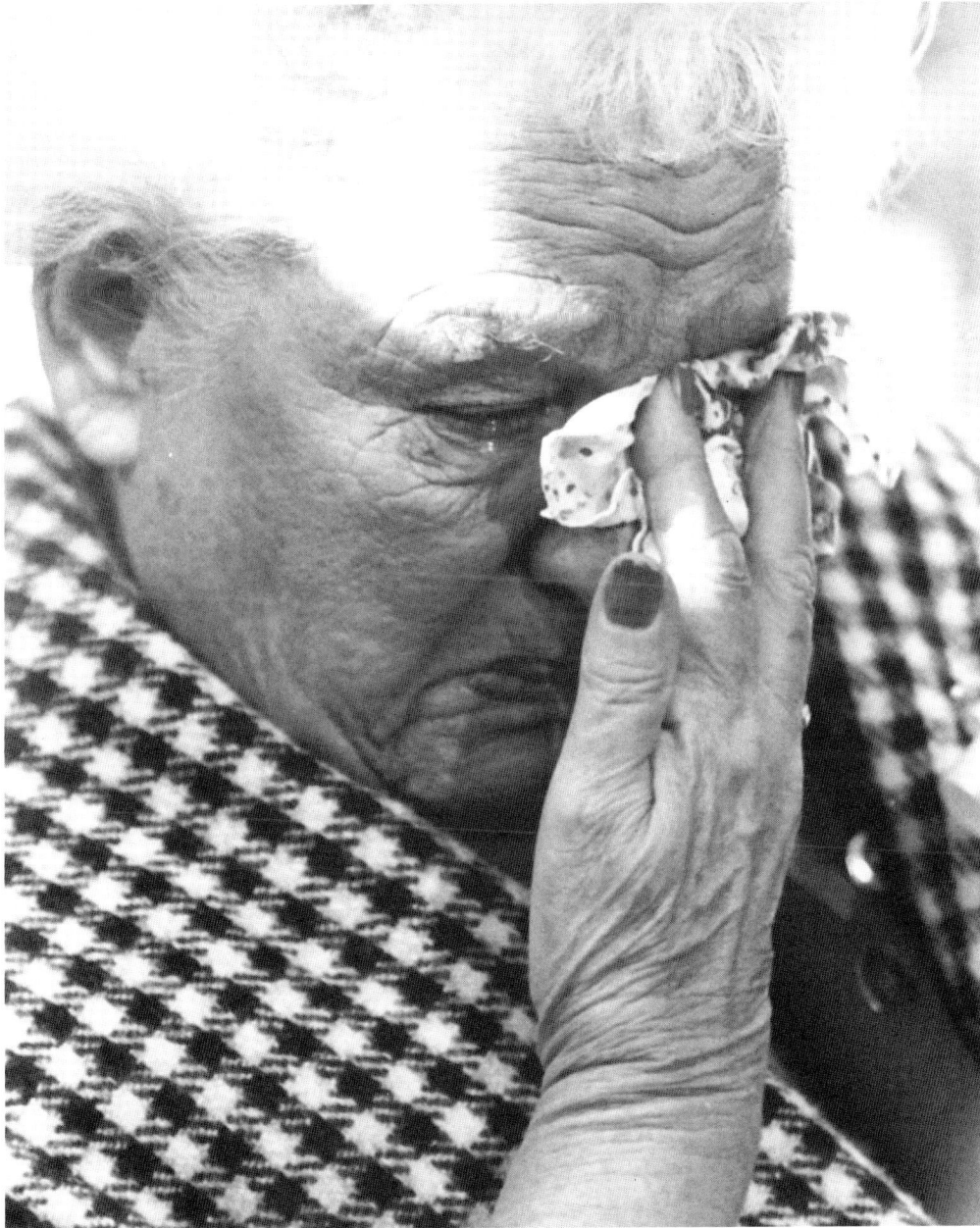

Some cry.

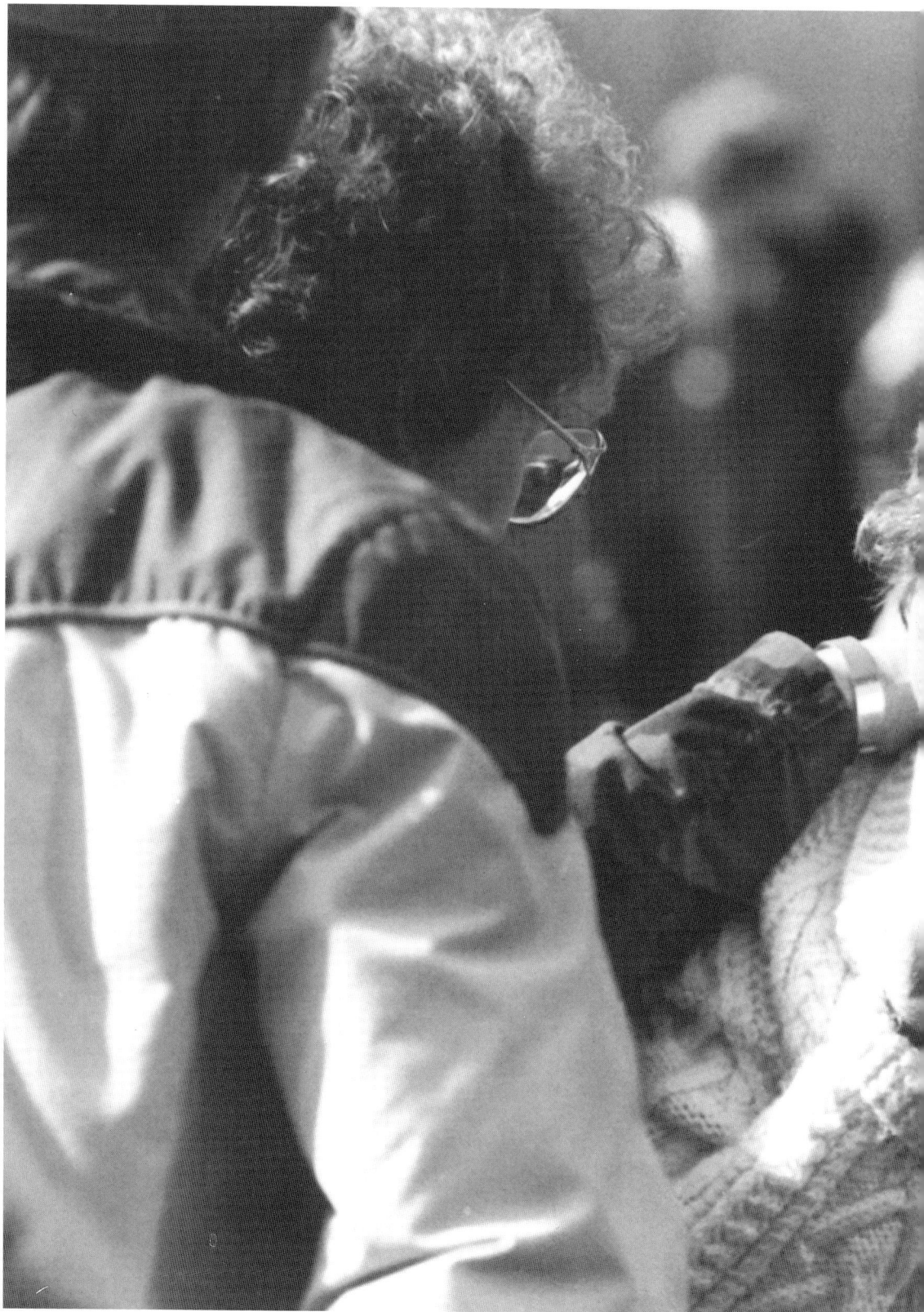

Some hug each other.

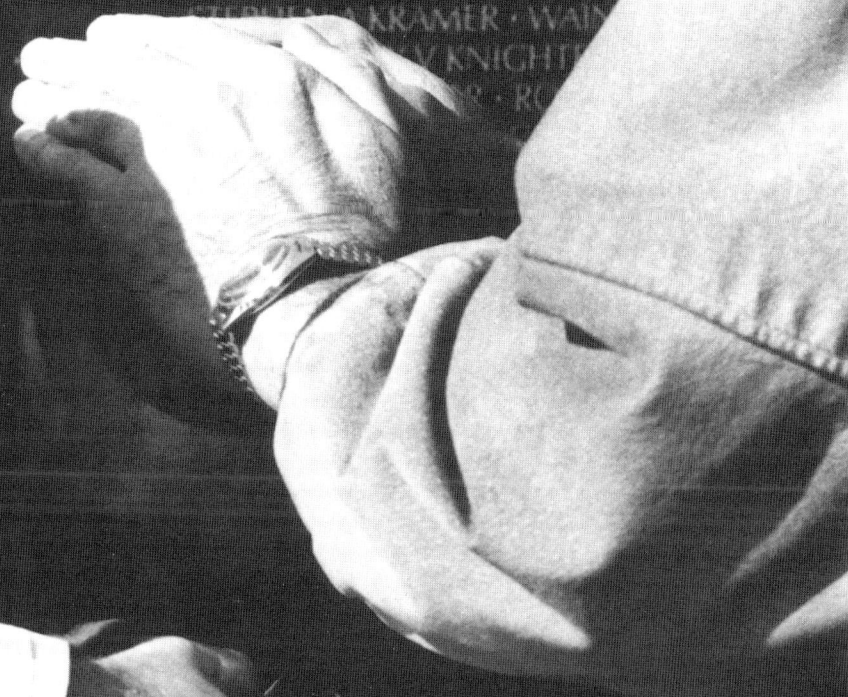

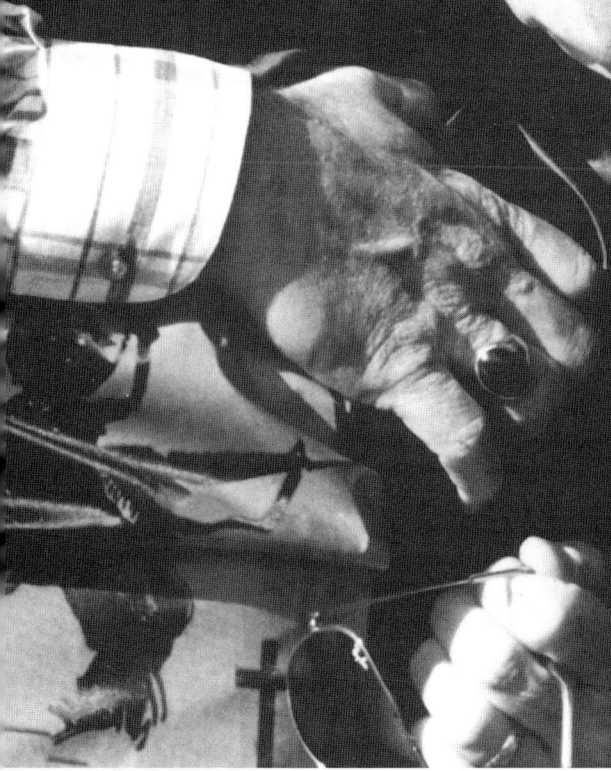

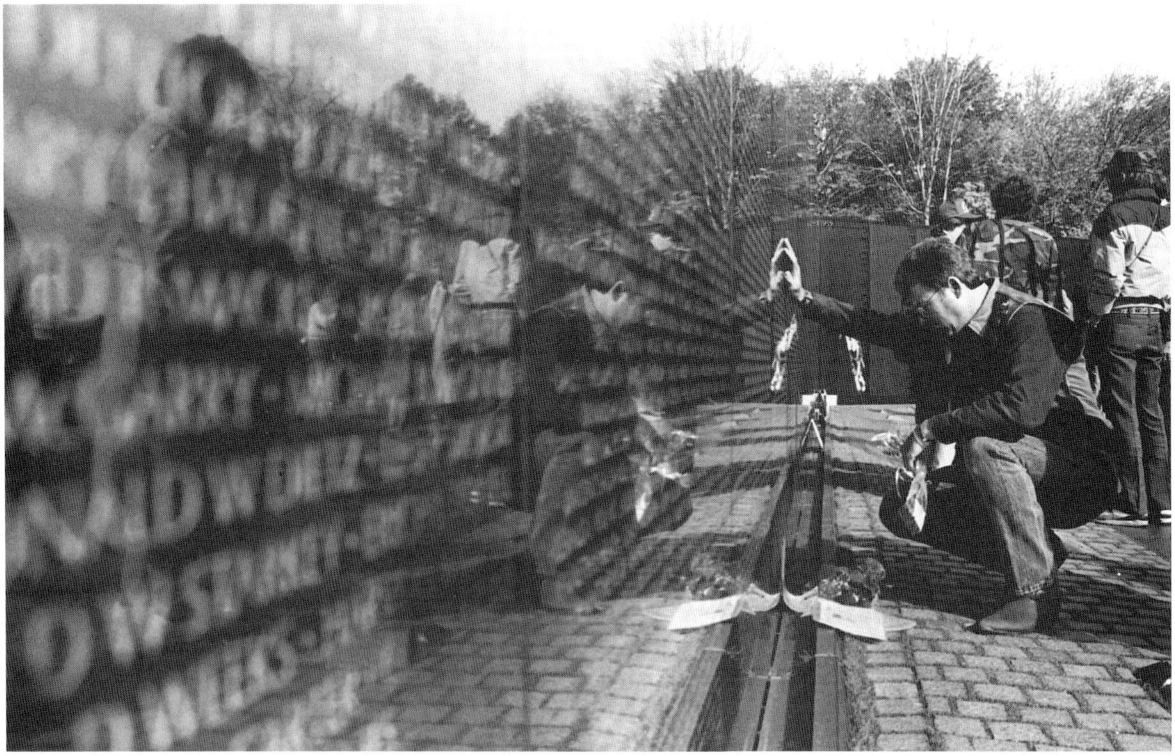

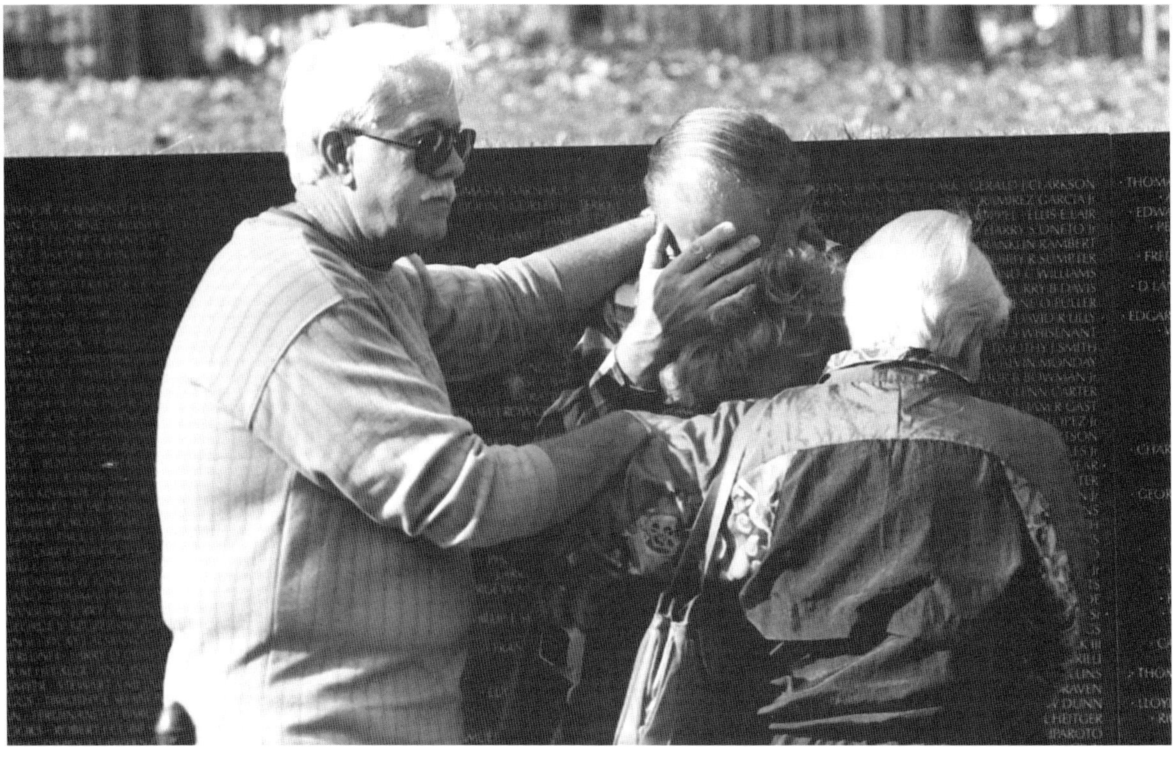

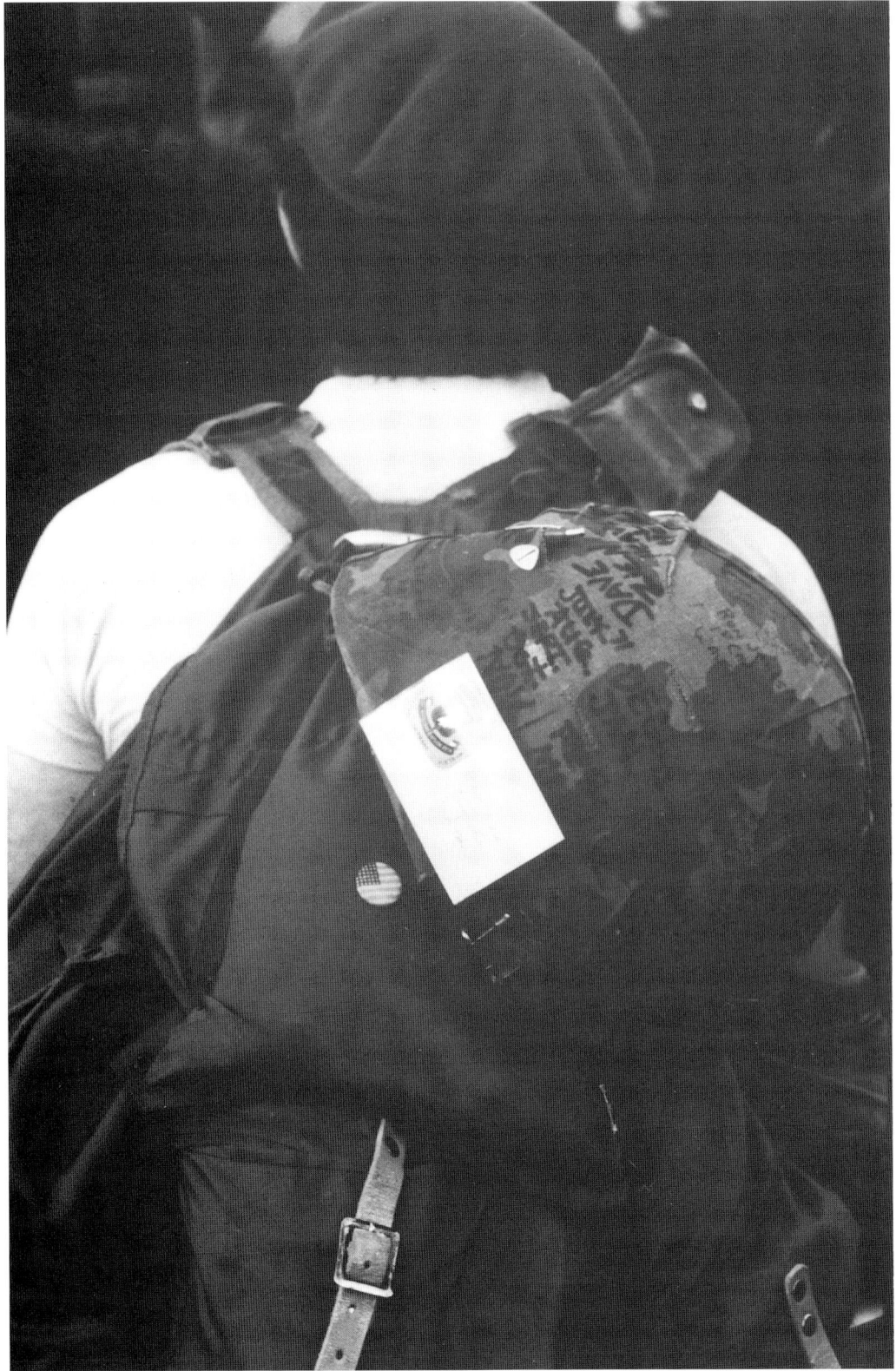

Some gather in small groups to talk and share stories of experiences from a bad place at a bad time.

Special ceremonies, Veterans Day or Memorial Day may bring thousands of visitors.

THANKS
67TH EVACUATION
HOSPITAL
6 SEPTEMBER 67

But on all the other days, the Mondays and Thursdays of our lives, there are hundreds of people who come. Some have husbands or fathers or sons or brothers or buddies who returned after serving in southeast Asia; some have family or friends who were wounded there; most know a name carved on the black granite.

Some visit with family or with friends to find their name. Some come alone to say good-by, or to pay their respects in the quiet of an evening.

Personal items are left there . . . a wreath, a picture, a letter, a stuffed animal, a can of beer for a fallen comrade, a medal earned but left to be shared by the buddy who really deserved it, a pair of worn jungle boots with the red dust of Vietnam still encrusted on them. All these years later, visitors still bring their memories, tied up in these small items, to the Wall.

My first visit was at a special time when there were thousands of veterans, their families and friends, all brothers and sisters, bound together, perhaps forever, by this unpopular war.

I have been back at quieter times. It is always emotional. No one walks away without feeling something.

For some veterans it takes years to deal with those feelings and visit the memorial. Some still haven't. They are afraid of letting those buried memories and their emotions surface. The majority of veterans I have talked with felt better after going, even if they had to force themselves as I did.

AM VETERANS

GANIZATION'S

ST VIGIL

Marines

It is a strange place, and everyone has a story when they go. One former combat medic took a picture of a name on the Wall. When he got the film, a cloud had appeared over the name of his fallen comrade - a cloud on a virtually cloudless day. Another friend talked of the sunny day he walked the path along the Wall. A fluke storm came up, the kind where you see it raining on one side of the road and the sun shining on the other. By the time he reached the other end, the rain had stopped. To him, it seemed the Wall was crying.

This book, with pictures of average people, like you and me, is a small part of the emotional path we've all traveled at the memorial. I hope they and all who come in the future, find what they are seeking.

I know I did.

Letting Go

"It's time for letting go!"
A voice cried out from "The Wall"
My Lt. was smiling,
it was his voice I heard call.

"These names reflect our deaths,
our lives ended years ago;
but you keep coming back
and why, we really don't know?"

"There's no need to feel guilt
and you mourned us when we died;
you've been here many times
and we watched as you cried.
You need to face the facts,
you were there when we checked out;

perhaps, we let you down
but Death would erase that doubt."
"If we could trade places,
would you want us to hold on?
We left our lives in Nam,
the pain of loss should be gone!"

C.M. Henderly

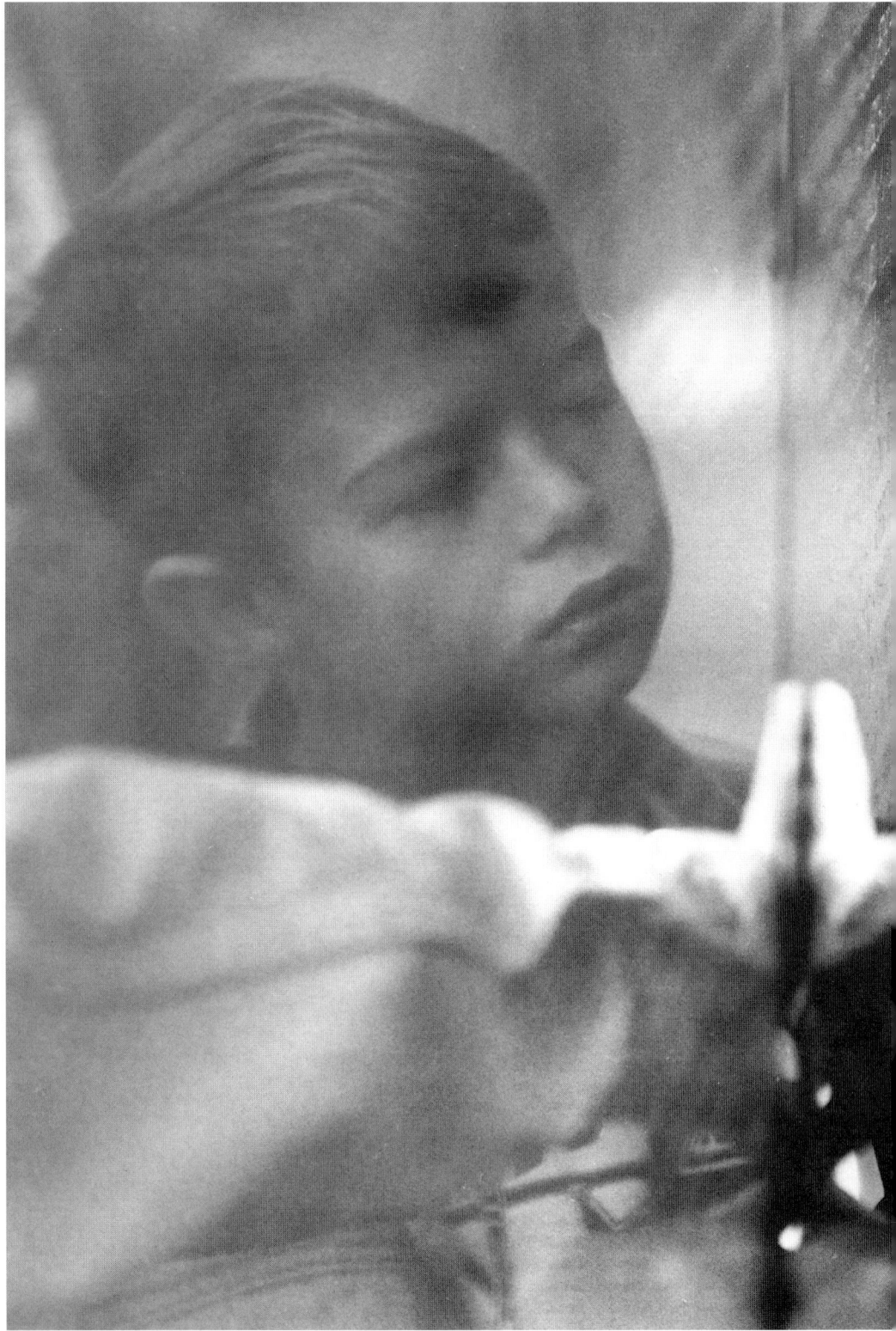